Minc

by

Carolyn Akens

Recipes for a Healthier Spirit, Soul and Body

ISBN 978-0-9882241-0-0

Mindful Meals: Recipes for a Healthier Spirit, Soul and Body
Carolyn Akens
P.O. Box 420644
Atlanta, Georgia 30342-0644

www.carolynakens.com

Cover photograph: Carolyn Akens

Print and eBook production: Marla Misch

Contents

Foreword

I have had the great fortune of knowing Carolyn Akens for more than a decade. As is so often now the case in our connected society, we met through the internet after my wife asked ever so sweetly that I conduct a search for a personal, family chef. Because our work and home schedules were becoming ever more hectic, we found ourselves relying more and more on take-out and other expensive, unhealthy choices for our dinners which were our best chance of the day to be together as a family. Not believing for one second that I could actually find someone of Carolyn's talent whom I could afford, I reluctantly started my search online. Now more than a decade later, Carolyn has become a dear and trusted friend to our family. We no longer view her as an exceptional chef, but rather as more of a health and lifestyle coach.

For the quarter century I have been blessed with an exceptional career as a brain and spine surgeon. I have spent countless hours both teaching and being taught the science of neurological surgery. An important part of this education has focused on how to properly nourish the patient after surgery to make the most of my repairs. Unfortunately the old saying about leading a horse to water comes to mind and represents an all-too-frequent complaint voiced by patients everywhere. If the building blocks we provide are not pleasing to the eye and palatable, then our efforts frequently fall short.

Personally I am a confirmed carnivore, and I view almost anything on my plate other than a succulent steak or chop as wasted space. My dear wife was patient early on in our marriage with my totally unhealthy and unbalanced approach to cuisine. In her infinite wisdom she gently tried to convince me that my choices came with a price. As is too often the case, her recommendations to balance my diet went largely unheeded. Enter Carolyn Akens.

When I first met Carolyn I asked her, as is my nature in a somewhat in-your-face manner, why I should hire her. She looked at me for a moment and smiled her amazing smile and very calmly and succinctly explained that she was also a magician. She would, with sleight of hand, prepare healthy foods in such a way that I and my hard-to-please children would clean our plates and ask for seconds. There were never thirds because the food was long gone.

Carolyn's approach is simple and if you trust her you will quickly realize a revelation in your approach to your diet. Everything she recommends has a well thought-out reason that makes perfect medical and nutritional sense. Don't get me started on how good it tastes!

Enjoy,

Charles O. Wood, M.D.

About Carolyn Akens

Carolyn became her first client years ago when she weighed 185 pounds. Her younger brother succumbed to morbid obesity at the age of 45 and left behind a wife, three children, and siblings. He had many health problems that were attributed to morbid obesity. After losing her brother, Carolyn knew she had to make some drastic changes.

Carolyn was in denial because her weight was evenly proportioned and had convinced herself that nothing was wrong. Given her height of 5' 4", weight of 185, and BMI of 31.8, she fell into the obese category. Reality quickly set in. Along with weight fluctuations, Carolyn was dealing with high cholesterol, migraines, and arthritis in her lower back. She discovered raw foods and knew that would be the beginning of her journey. She began juicing, drinking green smoothies, eating salads, and applying other techniques, all the while creating health and wellness, detox, and weight loss programs. She has used these programs for more than three years to maintain her weight loss and to keep her inner pipes clean and flowing.

During this life-changing event Carolyn lost an incredible 65 pounds and to this day has kept it off. Today she combines her knowledge as a Holistic Health Coach, Raw Food Educator, and Chef to provide her clients the same philosophy that she stands by.

"I believe in being true to myself and my clients. I am 80% raw and 20% cooked, which is clean vegan (no faux meat, which is processed and laden with gluten), and I share this with my clients openly." Carolyn believes in integrity in everything she says and does...and she looks and feels phenomenal!

Carolyn Akens is a Board Certified Holistic Health Coach, Raw Food Educator, Speaker, and Chef.

Acknowledgments

Sincere gratitude to my beloved late Grandmother, Mama Lizzie. Not only did you raise me, but because of you and your unwavering faith in God, I am doing what I was put here to do: prepare healing foods and educate the masses. I miss you and the seeds you planted in me continue to grow!

Marisa Wood, thank you for your encouragement. You battled cancer with faith and dignity! Continue to trust God and you will always WIN! You are a dear friend and a phenomenal woman!!

Karen Langston, thank you for giving me the support that I needed to complete this book. I appreciate you so much.

Marla Misch, thank you for working diligently to get this book created and set up. Blessings to you!

Thank you to all of my family and friends that supported me and continue to do so. You are too numerous to name, but I know who you are and I love you! God bless each of you abundantly!

Entrées, Soups & Sides

Neatballs with Puttanesca Sauce

Beets with Onion and Cumin

- 2 tablespoons unfiltered extra virgin olive oil
- 1 small onion, chopped
- 1 clove garlic, minced
- 1 1/2 teaspoons cumin seed
- 2 tablespoons brown rice flour
- 5 medium beets, peeled and quartered
- 2 tomatoes, peeled, seeded, and chopped
- 1 1/2 cups water
- 1 teaspoon Himalayan pink sea salt

Heat olive oil in a medium saucepan over medium-high heat; sauté onion and garlic until translucent. Mix in cumin seed and sauté an additional 2 minutes. Sprinkle in flour and sauté an additional minute.

Stir in beets, tomatoes, water, and salt. Decrease heat to low, cover pan with lid and simmer 30 to 45 minutes, until beets are tender.

Serves 4

Black Bean Cakes with Pineapple Salsa

- 1/4 cup organic coconut oil, divided
- 1 Vidalia onion, finely chopped
- 2 cans organic black beans, rinsed and drained
- 1 organic carrot, peeled and finely diced
- 1/4 cup finely diced organic red pepper
- 1/3 cup organic corn meal
- 1 tablespoon chili powder
- 1 tablespoon ground cumin
- 1 teaspoon Himalayan pink sea salt
- 1/4 teaspoon crushed red pepper flakes or a red jalapeño, finely chopped
- 1/2 cup finely chopped fresh organic cilantro
- 1/4 cup water

In a large stainless steel or iron skillet, heat 3 tablespoons of the coconut oil over medium heat. Add onions and cook until translucent. Put onions in large bowl. Save skillet for later use.

Add remaining ingredients to bowl of onions. Mash ingredients together using your hands or a spoon. If mixture feels dry add more water, one tablespoon at a time. Use a mold or your hands to form the ingredients into cakes, 2 inches in diameter.

Add the remaining oil to the skillet. Sauté for 2 to 3 minutes on each side until lightly browned.

Pineapple Salsa

- 1 cup diced fresh pineapple
- 1/4 cup finely diced cilantro
- 1/4 cup finely diced red onion
- Pinch of Himalayan pink sea salt

Combine all ingredients and serve over black bean cakes.

Serves 4-6

Black-Eyed Peas

Black-eyed Peas are my 'go to' food when I want a supple dish that I can eat as an entrée or side. They are also delicious in a salad. Black-eyed peas contain macronutrients, vitamins, and minerals. Not to be confused with the singing group, The Black Eyed Peas, although I can assure you that once you begin to eat them you will think that Will.i.am is singing to you.

- 1 package dried black-eyed peas
- 1 small sweet Vidalia onion, diced
- 1/2 teaspoon freshly ground black pepper
- 1 teaspoon Himalayan pink sea salt
- 3 cups organic vegetable broth
- 1/4 cup Earth Balance
- 1 teaspoon granulated garlic powder
- 1 teaspoon granulated onion powder
- 1/2 teaspoon chili pepper flakes
- 2 organic Roma tomatoes, diced
- 1 small red onion, diced

Soak black-eyed peas overnight. Drain, rinse, and cook in vegetable broth. Add the remaining ingredients, except tomatoes and red onion. Bring to a boil. Decrease heat and simmer for approximately 30-40 minutes.

Once cooked, garnish with the tomatoes and red onion.

Serves 6 to 8

Broccoli and Tomatoes with Tahini Dressing

- 1/4 cup tahini
- 2 oranges, juiced
- 1 tablespoon freshly squeezed lemon juice
- 3 heads organic broccoli
- 1/2 cup halved organic cherry tomatoes
- 1/4 teaspoon Himalayan pink sea salt
- 1/4 cup sliced almonds

Blend the tahini, orange and lemon juice in a Vitamix.

Shred the broccoli using the shredding blade in a food processor or slice with a knife.

Place the broccoli and halved tomatoes into a medium bowl. Pour the tahini dressing into the bowl and mix well.

Serve the broccoli and tomatoes, garnished with the almonds, on a plate.

Spicy Collard Greens

- 1-2 lbs. organic collards
- 1/2 red onion, diced
- 1/4 teaspoon red pepper flakes or cayenne pepper
- 1 teaspoon onion powder
- 1 teaspoon granulated garlic powder
- 1/2 teaspoon Himalayan pink sea salt
- 1/4 cup unfiltered extra virgin olive oil
- 2 lemons, juiced

Wash and rinse the greens thoroughly. Roll up the greens and cut them into chiffonade (small ribbons - this really makes a difference as they marinate).

Mix all ingredients in a bowl with your hands, squeezing gently until they have broken down.

Serves 4

Collard Wraps

- 5 medium to large collard leaves
- 1 heirloom tomato, sliced
- Alfalfa sprouts
- 1 carrot, shredded
- 1 avocado, peeled, pitted, and sliced
- 1 red onion, sliced
- Crimini mushrooms (optional)
- 1/4 cup wheat-free tamari
- 1/2 teaspoon lucuma powder (optional)
- 1/8 teaspoon Himalayan pink sea salt

Prepare the collard leaves by cutting off the stems at the base of the leaf, then take a small paring knife and carefully cut the thick bump of stem off the back of the leaf making it flush with the leaf.

Combine the carrot, onion, mushrooms, tamari, lucuma, and salt in a large mixing bowl.

Place a scoop of the mixture in the middle of the collard leaf. Lay the avocado, tomato, and alfalfa sprouts on the mixture. Roll up the leaf; continue with remaining leaves.

Serves 5

Corn Chowder

- 4 cups fresh organic corn kernels or frozen organic corn kernels, plus 1/4 cup, for garnish
- 2 cups almond milk
- 1 small avocado, peeled, pitted, and cut in chunks
- 1 teaspoon ground cumin
- 1/3 cup coarsely chopped Vidalia or red onion
- 1/2 teaspoon Himalayan pink sea salt
- 2 tablespoons nutritional yeast
- Chili oil drops, for garnish

Combine the corn (except for 1/4 cup), almond milk, avocado, cumin, chopped onion, nutritional yeast, and salt in a Vitamix; blend well.

Pour the soup into serving bowls. Garnish with corn kernels and chili oil.

Serves 4

Cream of Zucchini Soup

This creamy soup is delicious served chilled, at room temperature, or warmed gently on the stove or in the dehydrator.

- 1 cup filtered water, plus additional water to thin
- 2 medium organic zucchinis, peeled and chopped
- 2 stalks organic celery, chopped
- 2 tablespoons freshly squeezed lemon juice
- 2 tablespoons unfiltered extra virgin olive oil
- 2 teaspoons mellow white miso
- 2 small cloves garlic, crushed
- 1/2 teaspoon Himalayan pink sea salt (or to taste)
- 1/8 teaspoon cayenne pepper
- 1 avocado, peeled, pitted, and mashed
- 2 tablespoons minced fresh dill (or 2 teaspoons dried)

Combine the water, zucchini, celery, lemon juice, olive oil, miso, garlic, salt, and cayenne in a Vitamix; process until smooth. Add the avocado and dill; blend briefly. Add additional water to thin the soup to desired consistency and blend.

Serve chilled or at room temperature.

Daal

- 1 1/2 cups red lentils
- 1/4 cup unfiltered extra virgin olive oil
- 1 cup chopped red onion
- 1 1/2 teaspoons Himalayan pink sea salt
- 1 teaspoon ground turmeric
- 1 teaspoon ground cumin
- 1/4 teaspoon crushed red pepper
- 1/2 cup diced coriander leaves or Italian parsley
- Lemon peel, for garnish if desired

Cover lentils with water and soak 1 hour. Rinse thoroughly (rinsing the beans between soaking and cooking can reduce gastric disturbances).

Heat lentils and water to boiling. Cook 45 minutes, adding water if necessary. Drain lentils completely.

Heat oil in a 12-inch skillet. Stir in onion, salt, turmeric, cumin, and red peppers; cook over low heat until onion is tender. Set aside some of this mixture for garnish, if desired.

Garden Blend Soup

For variety, garnish soup with seasoned sunflower or pumpkin seeds, or top with salsa, fresh corn kernels, diced avocados, or tomatoes.

- 2 tablespoons freshly squeezed lemon juice
- 1/2 cup freshly squeezed orange juice or 1 apple, cored
- 1 cucumber
- 1/2 bunch parsley, washed thoroughly
- 1 avocado, peeled and pitted
- 1/2 bunch organic Romaine lettuce or other organic greens
- 1/4 bunch organic cilantro
- 1/4 bunch basil
- 1 tablespoon fresh dill
- 1 or 2 green onions, chopped, or 1 tablespoon chopped red onion
- 2 cloves garlic
- 1 1/2 cups filtered water
- 2 tablespoons mellow white miso
- 1/2 teaspoon Himalayan pink sea salt (or to taste)
- 1/2 red jalapeño pepper or dash cayenne pepper

Combine ingredients in Vitamix; puree until smooth.

Serves 4

Garlic Mashed Potatoes

Adapted from Recipe by Matthew Kenney

- 4 cups chopped jicama
- 2 cups cashews, soaked 1 hour
- 1 teaspoon Himalayan pink sea salt
- 3 cloves garlic, smashed
- 1 teaspoon granulated garlic powder
- 3 tablespoons almond milk
- 2 teaspoons nutritional yeast
- Black pepper, to taste

Process jicama in a food processor. Press out excess liquid through a nut milk bag or cheesecloth. Combine processed jicama with the remaining ingredients in a Vitamix; blend on high speed.

Serve immediately or warm in dehydrator before serving.

Gazpacho

This soup is delicious served chilled or at room temperature.

- 2 to 3 pounds organic heirloom or Roma tomatoes, coarsely chopped
- 1 stalk organic celery, coarsely chopped
- 1/2 organic cucumber, seeded, coarsely chopped
- 1/4 cup coarsely chopped organic bell pepper
- 1 organic green onion, chopped
- 1/4 bunch organic parsley, minced
- 4 organic radishes, thinly sliced
- 1 1/2 tablespoons freshly squeezed lemon juice
- 1/4 cup unfiltered extra virgin olive oil
- 1 teaspoon Himalayan pink sea salt
- 1/8 teaspoon freshly ground black pepper
- 1 avocado, peeled, pitted, and coarsely chopped
- 1/2 teaspoon chili oil
- 1 tablespoon ground cumin

Combine all ingredients, except chili oil, in a Vitamix until well-blended. Chill in the refrigerator. Drizzle with chili oil before serving.

Serves 4

Green Beans with Walnut Dijon Mustard Vinaigrette

Green Bean with Walnut Dijon Mustard Vinaigrette is an elegant side dish to serve to any one at any time. You can also use haricot verts, which are French green beans. ('Haricot' means beans and 'vert' means green - your French lesson for the day!)

- 2 pounds organic green beans
- 1/2 teaspoon Himalayan pink sea salt
- 1/4 teaspoon freshly ground white pepper

Blanch green beans in a pot of water with a rolling boil for 5 minutes; drain. Put into large bowl and add the vinaigrette and stir. Serve on a plate and top with walnuts.

Walnut Dijon Vinaigrette

- 1/2 cup walnut oil
- 2 tablespoons apple cider vinegar
- 3 tablespoons Dijon mustard
- 1 shallots, finely diced
- 1 teaspoon organic coconut nectar

Whisk or blend the ingredients and pour over green beans.

Serves 4

Green Peas with Orange Bell Pepper

Green Peas with Orange Bell Peppers is a quick and easy side that accompanies any entrée. Always keep organic green peas (aka sweet peas) in your freezer for a quick dish or to add to other side dishes. The colors pop and the aroma will awaken your senses!

- 2 pounds frozen organic green peas
- 1/3 cup diced orange bell pepper or 1/4 orange bell pepper, julienned
- 1/2 teaspoon Himalayan pink sea salt
- 1/4 teaspoon freshly ground black pepper
- 1 tablespoon Earth Balance

Add 1 pound of frozen green peas to a pot of water with a rolling boil; blanch for 5 minutes. Immediately place into an ice bath for one minute to stop the cooking process (retains the green color). Pour peas into a serving bowl and add the remaining ingredients and stir.

Serves 4

Guacamole

- 1 avocado, peeled, pitted, and mashed
- 1 organic plum tomato, juiced and seeded
- 1/3 cup chopped red onion
- 1/2 teaspoon chili powder
- 1/4 teaspoon cumin powder
- 1/8 teaspoon Himalayan pink sea salt
- 1 teaspoon minced cilantro

Combine all ingredients in a large bowl.

Italian Vegetable Rolls

- 1 cup chopped mushrooms
- 1 onion, chopped
- 1 cup sliced carrots
- 1 cup green peas
- 1 cup chopped broccoli
- 1 clove garlic, minced
- 1/4 cup red wine vinegar
- 1 cup shredded vegan mozzarella cheese
- 2 tablespoons unfiltered extra virgin olive oil
- 1/4 cup grated vegan Parmesan cheese
- 1 (16-ounce) package gluten-free lasagna noodles
- 26 ounces organic spaghetti sauce, Muir Glen

Cook noodles until al dente in a large pot of boiling water. Rinse, drain, set aside.

Heat oil in a medium sauté pan. Add mushrooms, onions, carrots, peas, and broccoli; sauté over medium heat until tender. Add red wine vinegar and garlic; cook 5 minutes. Remove from heat and cool for 10 minutes.

In a medium bowl combine sautéed vegetable mixture, mozzarella cheese, and 2 tablespoons Parmesan cheese; mix well.

Pour half of the sauce into the bottom of a 13 by 9 by 2-inch baking pan. Spread 1/3 cup vegetable mixture over each lasagna noodle then carefully roll up the noodle. Place seam side down in dish. When finished placing all the noodles in the pan, pour remaining pasta sauce evenly over noodles. Cover with aluminum foil.

Bake at 375° F (190° C) for 35 to 40 minutes. Uncover and sprinkle remaining Parmesan cheese over noodles. Bake, uncovered, 5 more minutes. Garnish and serve immediately.

Serves 4 to 6

Maple Eggplant Bacon

- 2 Japanese eggplants
- 2 tablespoons extra virgin olive oil
- 1 teaspoon wheat-free tamari
- 1/4 cup water
- 2 teaspoons smoked Spanish paprika
- 1 teaspoon ground Ancho chili pepper
- 2 tablespoon maple syrup

Peel the eggplants with a vegetable peeler. Slice the eggplant 1/8-inch thick using a mandolin, vegetable peeler, or sharp knife. Set aside.

Mix the marinade ingredients in a 9x13 glass dish. Place eggplant in marinade, cover completely, using the palm of your hand, press gently to ensure coverage. Cover and let stand for 1 hour.

Dehydrate at 115° for 24 hours or until your eggplant bacon is crispy.

Moroccan Couscous

This is a delicious dish that mimics the shape, texture, and taste of couscous. It can be chilled, served at room temperature, or warmed gently in a dehydrator.

- 1 head organic cauliflower
- 1/4 cup organic raisins
- 1/2 cup thinly sliced organic broccoli
- 1/4 cup thinly sliced organic carrots
- 1 to 2 organic parsnips, small dice
- 1/4 cup unsulfured sun-dried tomatoes
- 2 tablespoons goji berries
- 1/4 cup pine nuts

Marinade

- 1 tablespoon freshly squeezed lemon juice
- 2 tablespoons unfiltered extra virgin olive oil
- 1 tablespoon minced red onion
- 1 tablespoon dried oregano
- 1 tablespoon dried basil
- 1/4 teaspoon Himalayan pink sea salt
- 1/4 teaspoon freshly ground pepper
- 2 tablespoons curry
- 1 teaspoon turmeric
- 1/2 teaspoon lucuma powder
- 1 teaspoon Za'atar

Using the grater blade of a food processor, process cauliflower into grainy consistency. Combine the cut cauliflower with broccoli, carrots, sun-dried tomatoes, raisins, parsnips, pine nuts, and Goji berries in a bowl.

Combine the ingredients for marinade; pour over vegetable mixture. Toss well.

Serve at room temperature or slightly warmed in the dehydrator.

Serves 4

Neatballs with Puttanesca Sauce

- 2 cups soaked walnuts
- 2 tablespoons freshly squeezed lemon juice
- 2 teaspoons unfiltered extra virgin olive oil
- 2 teaspoons wheat-free tamari
- 2 teaspoons granulated garlic powder
- 1/2 teaspoon Himalayan pink sea salt
- 2 tablespoons coarsely chopped Italian parsley
- 2 tablespoons coarsely chopped red onions
- 1 tablespoon Italian seasoning

Combine the walnuts, lemon juice, olive oil, tamari, garlic powder, and salt in a food processor; process into a pâté, scraping the sides of the bowl with a spatula. Transfer the pâté to a mixing bowl and add the remaining three ingredients and mix well. Form neatballs and place in bowl.

Puttanesca Sauce

- 1/2 cup organic sun-dried tomatoes
- 1 cup organic Roma tomatoes, seeded
- 2 tablespoons Kalamata olives
- 2 tablespoons unfiltered extra virgin olive oil
- 1/4 cup coarsely chopped red onions
- 2 cloves garlic
- 2 tablespoons organic Italian parsley
- 1 teaspoon dried oregano
- 1 teaspoon dried basil
- 1 teaspoon dried thyme
- 1/8 teaspoon chili pepper flakes
- 1/2 teaspoon Himalayan pink sea salt
- 1/2 teaspoon freshly ground black pepper

Combine all ingredients in a Vitamix; blend until smooth.

Pour sauce over neatballs and serve.

Keep in the refrigerator for up to five days.

Serves 2-3

Pasta Primavera

- 12 ounces gluten-free spaghetti or linguine
- 1/2 small bunch of broccoli, cut into 1-inch pieces (about 2 cups)
- Unfiltered extra virgin olive oil or gluten-free organic vegetable broth, to sauté vegetables
- 12 ounces halved mushrooms
- 1 small onion, minced
- 1 small carrot, cut into julienne slices
- 1 small red pepper, cut into 1/4-inch thick strips
- 8 ounces almond milk
- 1/2 cup gluten-free organic vegetable broth
- 1 1/2 teaspoons sweet rice flour
- 1/2 teaspoon Himalayan pink sea salt
- 2 cloves garlic, minced
- 1 medium-sized organic Roma tomato, seeded and diced
- 3 tablespoons shredded vegan mozzarella cheese
- 2 tablespoons minced parsley

Cook pasta as directed on label in a large saucepan. Drain and return to saucepan; keep warm.

Meanwhile, in 2-quart saucepan over high heat, add broccoli pieces to 1 inch of boiling water; return to a boil, cover, and decrease heat to low. Simmer 2-3 minutes, stirring once or twice, until tender-crisp. Drain.

Preheat a 12-inch skillet over high heat. When hot, add broth, garlic, onion and carrot; stir frequently, until golden and tender-crisp. Add red pepper and mushrooms and cook, stirring, until vegetables are tender.

In a 2-cup measuring cup, mix almond milk, broth, rice flour, and salt. Blend well with a fork, until all the lumps are dissolved.

Stir the milk mixture into the vegetable mixture in skillet. Bring to a boil over high heat; cook one minute. Add tomato, cheese, parsley, broccoli, and pasta, tossing to coat all with sauce; heat through.

Serves 6

Spicy-Cheesy Kale Chips

Sauce

- 1/3 cup water
- 2 cloves garlic
- 2 tablespoons freshly squeezed lemon juice
- 1 cup seeded and coarsely chopped red or orange bell pepper
- 1/2 cup ground flax seeds
- 1/4 cup nutritional yeast flakes
- 1 tablespoon chili powder
- 2 teaspoons wheat-free tamari
- 1 teaspoon Himalayan pink sea salt
- 1 teaspoon granulated garlic powder
- 1/2 teaspoon cayenne pepper or chili oil
- 1 tablespoon turmeric powder

Combine all ingredients for the sauce in a Vitamix; blend until smooth and creamy.

De-stem one bunch of Lacinato (dinosaur kale) or curly kale and tear into half or pieces (depends on the size of the chips you want). Using your hands, mix the kale into the cheese sauce; coat the kale thoroughly with the sauce.

Arrange the kale in one layer on ParaFlexx sheets and dehydrate on 145° for 2 hours and then dehydrate on 115 for desired crispiness.

Spinach Apple Soup

- 1 cup filtered water
- 1 1/2 Gala apples, peeled and chopped
- 1 cup spinach leaves
- 1 zucchini, chopped
- 1 teaspoon freshly squeezed lemon juice
- 1/2 avocado, peeled, pitted, and chopped
- 1/8 teaspoon Himalayan pink sea salt

Combine all ingredients in a Vitamix; blend until smooth.

Serves 2

Sunflower Pâté

- 3 cups sunflower seeds, soaked 4 hours
- 1/2 cup freshly squeezed lemon juice
- 1/4 cup diced red onion
- 1/3 cup raw tahini
- 1/3 cup wheat-free tamari
- 1/2 cup coarsely chopped sweet Vidalia onions
- 2 tablespoons chopped parsley
- 2 cloves garlic
- 1/2 teaspoon cayenne pepper
- 1 teaspoon ground cumin

Combine all ingredients in a food processor; process into a smooth paste.

Roasted Curried Sweet Potatoes

Did you know that North Carolina produces more sweet potatoes than any other state? Sweet potatoes are rich in complex carbohydrates, dietary fiber, and beta-carotene. When the curry is added to the sweet potatoes, they do a happy dance in your mouth!

- 1/4 cup Earth Balance or unfiltered extra virgin olive oil
- 1 tablespoon Madras curry powder
- 1 tablespoon coconut nectar
- 1 teaspoon cinnamon
- 1/4 teaspoon Himalayan pink sea salt
- 1 pound sweet potatoes, peeled and cut into 1-inch pieces

Preheat oven to 450° F.

In a small saucepan melt Earth Balance and stir in curry powder, salt, cinnamon, and coconut nectar.

In a large bowl, toss potatoes with Earth Balance mixture; pour onto baking sheet.

Roast for 30-45 minutes until browned.

Serves 4

Vegan Chili

- 1 cup dried red kidney beans (or organic canned kidney beans)
- 1 tablespoon extra virgin coconut oil
- 1 large onion, finely chopped
- 3 cloves garlic, minced
- 1 large red bell pepper, medium dice
- 1 large yellow bell pepper, medium dice
- 2 cups medium dice butternut squash
- 2 tablespoons cacao powder or organic cocoa powder
- 1 tablespoon coconut nectar
- 1 teaspoon dried marjoram
- 1/2 teaspoon Himalayan pink or Celtic sea salt
- 1 1/2 cups canned crushed tomatoes
- 1/4 teaspoon chili flakes
- 1 teaspoon chili powder
- 1 teaspoon ground cumin

Cover the kidney beans with water in a large saucepan; bring to a boil. Decrease heat to simmer and cook for 2 to 2 1/2 hours, or until beans are tender. Drain the beans, reserving one cup of the liquid.

Heat the oil over medium heat in a Dutch oven. Add the onion and garlic; cook until tender (about 7 minutes). Stir in the bell peppers and butternut squash; cook for 4 minutes or until the peppers are crisp-tender. Add the cacao, coconut nectar, marjoram, chili flakes, chili powder, cumin, and salt, stirring to coat.

Stir in the drained beans, reserved liquid, and tomatoes; bring to a boil. Decrease to a simmer; cover and cook for 30 minutes to meld the flavors.

Serves 4

Herb Roasted Vegetables

- 1 1/2 pounds sweet potatoes, quartered
- 1/2 cup baby carrots
- 1 small red onion, cut into wedges
- 1/4 cup unfiltered extra virgin olive oil
- 3 tablespoons freshly squeezed lemon juice
- 3 cloves garlic, minced
- 1 tablespoon chopped fresh rosemary
- 1 tablespoon dried oregano
- 1/2 teaspoon Himalayan pink sea salt
- 1/2 teaspoon freshly ground black pepper
- 1/2 small eggplant, quartered and cut into 1/2-inch slices
- 1 red bell pepper, cut into 1/2-inch wide strips

Preheat oven to 450° F (230° C).

Combine potatoes, carrots, and onion in an ungreased 13 by 9-inch baking pan. Combine extra virgin olive oil, lemon juice, garlic, rosemary, oregano, salt, and pepper to taste in a small mixing bowl. Drizzle the mixture over the vegetables. Bake for 20 minutes.

Remove the baking dish from the oven and add eggplant and bell pepper. Toss to combine the eggplant and bell pepper with the other vegetables. Return the pan to the oven and bake for 13 to 15 more minutes, or until the vegetables are tender and brown on the edges. Serve hot.

Serves 4 to 6

Roasted Vegetables

Roasting vegetables bring out the natural sweetness. You can taste each vegetable and enjoy the suppleness of each and every one.

- 2 sweet potatoes, peeled and cubed
- 4 carrots, sliced diagonally
- 1 head fresh broccoli, cut into florets
- 4 zucchinis, sliced diagonally
- 1/2 teaspoon Himalayan pink sea salt
- 1 tablespoon organic extra virgin coconut oil
- 1 teaspoon dried organic Italian seasoning

Preheat oven to 400° F (205 ° C). Lightly grease a large baking dish with organic extra virgin coconut oil.

Toss vegetables in bowl with salt, seasoning, and organic extra virgin coconut oil until well coated. Pour into the baking dish.

Bake for 30 to 45 minutes or until vegetables are tender.

Serves 4

Vegetable Quinoa

Quinoa is not a grain, but a seed that is gluten-free and very good for you. Quinoa is a protein powerhouse; excellent for weight loss; cleanser and detoxifier; plant derived calcium; and brain food! Add vegetables and you're in for a delicious meal.

- 1 cup organic quinoa, rinsed
- 2 cups organic vegetable broth
- 1/3 cup diced yellow onion
- 1/3 cup diced organic carrots
- 1/3 cup organic sweet peas
- 1/3 cup organic corn
- 1 teaspoon Himalayan pink sea salt
- 1 teaspoon freshly ground black pepper
- 1 teaspoon granulated garlic powder
- 1 teaspoon onion powder

Add all ingredients, except green peas, to a sauté pan and bring to a boil. Decrease heat, cover pan with a lid, and simmer until quinoa is tender, but chewy, and white spiral like threads appear around each grain, about 15 minutes. Add the green peas. Stir, fluff, and serve.

Serves 4

Salads and Dressings

Apple Spinach Cabbage Slaw

Dressing

- 1/4 cup almonds, soaked in water for 8 hours
- 2 tablespoons unfiltered organic olive oil
- 1 tablespoon freshly squeezed lemon juice
- 1 tablespoon mellow white miso
- 1 clove garlic, crushed
- 1 tablespoon coconut nectar
- 1 teaspoon onion powder
- 1/4 teaspoon dry mustard powder
- 1/8 teaspoon Himalayan pink sea salt
- 1/3 cup filtered water

Salad

- 1/2 bunch baby spinach, washed
- 1 small organic head cabbage, shredded
- 1 organic Roma tomato, diced
- 1/2 cup leeks or green onion, thinly sliced
- 1 Pink Lady apple, julienned
- 1 Granny Smith apple, thinly sliced

Combine the ingredients for dressing in a Vitamix and puree until the consistency of vinaigrette. Toss with spinach, cabbage, tomato, leeks, and Pink Lady apple. Place thinly sliced Granny Smith apples on plate and place salad mixture on top.

Bulgur Chick Pea Salad

- 1 cup bulgur
- 2 cups boiling water
- 1/2 cup unfiltered extra virgin olive oil
- 1/2 cup freshly squeezed lemon juice
- 1/2 teaspoon Himalayan pink sea salt
- 1/2 teaspoon freshly ground black pepper
- 1 cup chopped green onions
- 1 (15-ounce) can organic garbanzo beans, rinsed and drained
- 1 cup chopped fresh Italian parsley
- 1 cup grated carrots

In a heatproof bowl, pour boiling water over bulgur. Let stand 1 hour at room temperature.

In a small bowl, beat together oil, lemon juice, salt, and pepper. Pour over bulgur and mix with a fork.

Place bulgur in the bottom of a glass-serving bowl. Layer vegetables and garbanzo beans in this order on top of the bulgur: green onions, garbanzo beans, parsley, and carrots on top. Cover and refrigerate.

Toss salad before serving.

Serves 7

Cabbage Cilantro Slaw

- 1 small head of cabbage, finely shredded
- 1 small onion, minced
- 2 tablespoons minced fresh cilantro
- 1 English cucumber

Mix cabbage, onion, and cilantro.

Peel and seed cucumber; cut into 3-inch sticks.

Cover and refrigerate cabbage mixture and cucumber separately for up to 24 hours. Prepare Lime and Garlic Dressing.

Lime and Garlic Dressing

- 1/2 cup unfiltered extra virgin olive oil
- 1/3 cup freshly squeezed lime juice
- 2 cloves garlic, minced or pressed

Whisk oil, lime juice, and garlic. Pour dressing into cabbage mixture, pile into serving platter. Garnish with cucumber. Season with salt and pepper.

Serves 4

Chick Pea Macaroni Salad

- 1 cup uncooked gluten-free macaroni pasta
- 1 (19-ounce) can garbanzo beans, rinsed and drained
- 4 tomatoes, chopped
- 1 red onion, chopped
- 1 clove garlic, minced
- 6 ounces vegan Parmesan cheese
- 1 cup pitted black olives
- 1 teaspoon Himalayan pink sea salt
- 1/2 teaspoon freshly ground black pepper
- 1/3 cup unfiltered extra virgin olive oil
- 1/4 cup freshly squeezed lemon juice

Cook pasta until al dente in a large pot of salted boiling water. Drain and rinse under cold water.

In a large bowl, combine the pasta, chickpeas, tomatoes, onion, garlic, cheese, olives, salt, pepper, olive oil, and lemon juice. Toss together and refrigerate until chilled.

Serves 4 to 6

Corn, Black Bean, & Red Pepper Salad

- 2 cups organic corn kernels, fresh or frozen
- 16 ounces organic black beans
- 1 organic red bell pepper, diced
- 4 tablespoons unfiltered extra virgin olive oil
- 2 tablespoons white wine vinegar
- 1/2 teaspoon ground cumin
- Salt and pepper to taste
- 2 tablespoons chopped cilantro

Combine all ingredients, except cilantro, in large bowl; mix well. Sprinkle with cilantro.

Serves 4

Cucumber and Avocado Salad

- 1 English cucumber
- 1/8 teaspoon Himalayan pink sea salt
- Chili pepper
- 1 tablespoon freshly squeezed lime juice
- 1 teaspoon minced onion
- 1 red chili pepper, sliced
- Butter lettuce
- 1 avocado, peeled, pitted, and sliced
- Fresh Italian parsley

Peel and slice the cucumber paper-thin. Season with salt, chili pepper, and lime juice. Sprinkle with onion and red pepper slices.

Arrange lettuce on serving plates. Add cucumber mixture. Top with avocado and parsley.

Serves 1 to 3

Cucumber-Mint Salad

- 1 large English cucumber
- 1 small red onion, finely chopped
- 1 tablespoon chopped fresh mint
- 1/4 cup white wine vinegar
- 1 teaspoon coconut nectar
- 1/2 teaspoon Himalayan pink sea salt
- 1/2 teaspoon lemon pepper seasoning

Peel cucumber and chop into 1/4-inch cubes.

Combine all ingredients in bowl and mix. Serve at room temperature.

Serves 1 to 2

Egg-less Egg Salad

- 1/2 cup water
- 1/3 cup freshly squeezed lemon juice
- 2 teaspoons turmeric
- 2 cloves garlic, peeled
- 1 teaspoon onion powder
- 1/4 teaspoon mustard powder
- 1 teaspoon Himalayan pink sea salt
- 1 1/2 cups cashews
- 1/3 cup chopped scallions
- 1/3 cup chopped celery
- 1/3 cup chopped red bell pepper

Combine the water, lemon juice, turmeric, onion powder, mustard powder, garlic, salt, and cashews in a food processor; blend until smooth.

In a medium mixing bowl, combine the contents of the food processor with the scallions, celery, and bell pepper. Mix well and serve.

Jicama Potato Salad

Adapted from recipe by Matthew Kenney

- 2 cups diced jicama
- 1/4 cup diced organic yellow pepper
- 1/4 cup diced organic celery
- 2 tablespoons minced green olives (optional)
- 1/4 cup avocado, pitted and mashed
- 1/2 red onion, thinly sliced

In a bowl, combine all the ingredients and set aside.

Jicama Potato Salad Dressing

- 3 tablespoons tahini
- 1/4 teaspoon ground cumin
- 2 tablespoons freshly squeezed lemon juice
- 3 tablespoons filtered water
- 2 teaspoons fresh parsley
- 1/4 teaspoon wheat-free tamari
- 1/4 teaspoon lucuma
- 1/8 teaspoon Himalayan pink sea salt
- 1/8 teaspoon chili powder
- 1/8 teaspoon turmeric
- 1/8 teaspoon ground mustard

Combine all ingredients for the dressing in a Vitamix; blend until smooth.

Pour the dressing over salad and toss until combined and serve.

Serves 2-3

Mexican Green Bean Salad

- 1 pound organic green beans
- 1/2 cup unfiltered extra virgin olive oil
- 2 red jalapeño peppers, seeded and chopped
- 1 tablespoon red wine vinegar
- 2 tablespoons freshly squeezed lemon juice
- 1 tablespoon minced yellow onion
- 1 tablespoon minced Italian parsley
- 1 tablespoon minced fresh cilantro

Steam green beans until crisp tender, about 15 minutes. Drain.

Whisk together other ingredients and pour over warm green beans. Allow to marinate at least 1/2 hour.

Serve at room temperature or chilled.

Serves 4

Raspberry & Avocado Grapefruit Salad

- Bibb lettuce
- Watercress
- 2 avocados, peeled, pitted, and sliced
- 2 cups grapefruit sections
- 1 cup fresh raspberries

Prepared sweet vinegar and oil dressing

Line salad plates with lettuce and watercress. Arrange avocado, grapefruit, and raspberries; sprinkle with Sweet Vinegar & Oil Dressing.

Sweet Vinegar & Oil Dressing

- 1/3 cup unfiltered extra virgin olive oil
- 2 tablespoons coconut nectar
- 1/4 cup white wine vinegar
- 1 teaspoon freshly squeezed lemon juice

Combine all ingredients.

Serves 4

Six-Bean Salad

- 1/2 cup coconut nectar
- 1/2 teaspoon Himalayan pink sea salt
- 1 cup apple cider vinegar
- 16 ounces organic green beans
- 16 ounces organic yellow beans
- 16 ounces organic lima beans
- 16 ounces organic garbanzo beans
- 16 ounces organic red kidney beans
- 16 ounces organic black beans
- 1 red bell pepper, diced
- 4 celery sticks, sliced
- 3 medium red onions, thinly sliced

Combine coconut nectar, salt, and vinegar in pan, bring to boil for 1 minute; let cool.

Mix all other ingredients together in a large bowl; add vinegar mixture. Marinate for 24 hours in refrigerator, stirring occasionally.

Serves 6 to 8

Tomato Squash Salad

- 1 pound small yellow squash or zucchini, or combination of both, sliced diagonally
- 1 pound small, ripe tomatoes, cut in wedges
- 1/2 cup sliced narrow strips red onion
- 1/4 cup packed fresh basil leaves
- 1/4 cup white wine vinegar
- 1 1/2 teaspoons unfiltered extra virgin olive oil
- 1 clove garlic, minced
- 1/4 teaspoon Himalayan pink sea salt
- 1/4 teaspoon freshly ground black pepper

Arrange squash in a steamer over boiling water. Cover and steam 1 minute, then plunge into cold water to stop the cooking. Drain well.

Combine squash, tomatoes, onion, and basil in salad bowl.

In a small bowl combine the remaining ingredients. Pour over the vegetables and toss gently.

Serve chilled or at room temperature.

Serves 4 to 6

Spinach Salad with Pears and Cranberries

- 1 teaspoon finely shredded orange peel
- 1/2 cup freshly squeezed orange juice
- 1/4 cup rice vinegar
- 1/3 cup dried unsulfured cranberries
- 2 firm, ripe pears
- 3/4 cup thinly sliced red onion
- 1 pound baby spinach, rinsed, crisped

Combine orange peel, orange juice, vinegar, and cranberries.

Core and slice pears. Add pears and onion to dressing. Pour over spinach immediately before serving. Mix gently.

Serves 4

24-Hour Slaw

- 1/2 cup coconut nectar
- 1 large head of cabbage, shredded
- 2 large red onions, thinly sliced
- Hot dressing (see below)

Stir brown rice syrup into cabbage except one teaspoon.

Place half the cabbage in a large bowl. Cover with onion slices. Top with remaining cabbage.

Pour boiling hot dressing (below) over slowly. Do not stir. Cover and refrigerate immediately. Chill for 24 hours. Stir well before serving.

Hot Dressing

- 1 teaspoon celery seeds
- 1 teaspoon coconut nectar
- 1 teaspoon dry mustard
- 1 1/2 teaspoon Himalayan pink sea salt
- 1 cup apple cider vinegar
- 1/2 cup unfiltered extra virgin olive oil

Combine celery seeds, coconut nectar, mustard, salt, and vinegar in saucepan. Bring to a rolling boil. Stirring, add oil and return to rolling boil.

Serves 4 to 6

Caesar Dressing

- 1/4 cup unfiltered extra virgin olive oil
- 2 cloves garlic
- 1/4 cup freshly squeezed lemon juice
- 2 teaspoons of dulse flakes
- 10 almonds, soaked
- 1/2 teaspoon Himalayan pink sea salt
- 2 soft Barhi or Medjool dates, pitted
- 1/8 teaspoon cayenne pepper
- 1 teaspoon garlic powder
- 1 cup water

Combine all ingredients in a Vitamix and blend until smooth. Store in a glass jar in the refrigerator for up to two weeks.

Creamy Citrus Dressing

- 1 small avocado, peeled and pitted
- 1 cup freshly squeezed orange juice
- 1/4 cup freshly squeezed lime juice
- 1 handful cilantro
- 1 green onion, coarsely chopped in entirety
- 1/8 teaspoon cayenne pepper
- 1/2 teaspoon Himalayan pink sea salt
- 1/2 cup unfiltered extra virgin olive oil
- Freshly ground black pepper

Combine the avocado, orange and lime juices, cilantro, green onion, cayenne, and salt in a Vitamix; blend until smooth. With the Vitamix running, slowly pour in the olive oil, allowing it to emulsify for a thick, creamy consistency. Season the dressing with pepper.

Orange Mango Dressing

- 1/2 cup freshly squeezed orange juice
- 1/2 cup mango
- 2 tablespoons unfiltered extra virgin olive oil
- 1 tablespoon coconut nectar
- 1/2 lemon, juiced
- 1/2 teaspoon tahini
- 1/8 teaspoon cayenne pepper (optional)
- Pinch of Himalayan pink sea salt

Combine all ingredients in a Vitamix; blend until smooth.

Tzatziki

- 2 organic English cucumbers, peeled, seeded, and quartered
- 1 tablespoon Himalayan pink sea salt
- 4 cloves garlic, minced
- 1 tablespoon freshly squeezed lemon juice
- 1 1/2 cups coconut milk yogurt, dairy-free (So Delicious brand)
- 1 teaspoon white wine vinegar
- 1/4 cup unfiltered extra virgin olive oil

Place quartered cucumbers in a small colander and sprinkle evenly with salt. Allow to drain for 30 minutes. Pat dry with paper towels and chop coarsely in food processor. Drain cucumber in colander for an additional 30 minutes.

Place cucumber back in food processor with garlic, lemon juice, yogurt, and vinegar. Blend well. Adjust vinegar and salt to taste. Pour in olive oil and blend until ingredients are well combined. Refrigerate until ready to serve.

Serves 8

Desserts, Breads & Goodies

Coconut Pineapple Cupcakes

Almond Butter

- 2 cups almonds
- 1 tablespoon coconut nectar (optional)
- 1/4 teaspoon Himalayan pink sea salt

Process the almonds in food processor for 13 minutes. Do not add the coconut or salt as it causes the almond butter to seize. Once the process begins, scrape down the sides. At first the mixture will become a powdery substance; continue processing for 10 minutes. Next the mixture will form a 'ball'; continue to process. Finally it will turn 'doughy' and then buttery smooth.

Pour the almond butter into a bowl. Add the coconut nectar, salt, and stir.

Store in the refrigerator for two weeks.

Almond Milk

Almond milk is a delicious non-diary drink that is delicious. It is easy to digest, so those who are lactose intolerant have a great alternative.

- 1 cup whole raw almonds
- 2 1/2 cups water
- 3 pitted Barhi or Medjool dates, soaked in water
- 1/2 teaspoon pure vanilla extract (optional)

Soak raw almonds in water for 8 hours or overnight; drain and rinse (yields 1 1/2 cups).

Add water, almonds, dates, and vanilla together in a Vitamix. Blend on high speed until smooth. To separate the "milk" from the almond pulp, squeeze the blended mixture through a nut milk bag or double layer of cheesecloth. Serve chilled or at room temperature.

Store in the refrigerator for up to five days; shake it before using.

Makes 2 1/2 cups milk.

Cashew Mayonnaise

- 1 cup cashews, soaked
- 1/4 cup water
- 1/4 cup freshly squeezed lemon juice
- 2 Barhi or Medjool dates, pitted
- 1 teaspoon onion powder
- 1/2 teaspoon mustard powder
- 1/2 teaspoon garlic powder
- 1 teaspoon Himalayan pink sea salt
- 1 dash white pepper
- 1/2 cup unfiltered extra virgin olive oil
- 1/4 cup raw pine nuts

Combine all ingredients, except the oil, in a Vitamix and blend until smooth. Add the oil in a steady stream while continuing to blend until the mayonnaise is emulsified.

Store in a tightly sealed container in the refrigerator for up to two weeks.

Cashew Sour Cream

- 1 cup raw cashews, soaked 1 hour
- 1/4 teaspoon Himalayan pink sea salt
- 1/4 cup filtered water
- 1 teaspoon apple cider vinegar
- 2 tablespoons freshly squeezed lemon juice (add more if needed)

Combine all ingredients in a food processor; puree until smooth and creamy in consistency.

Chocolate Banana Mousse Torte

- 1 cup shredded dry coconut
- 1 cup macadamia nuts, cashews, almonds, hazelnuts, etc.
- 1/4 cup packed pitted dates
- 1/2 teaspoon Himalayan pink sea salt
- 1/8 teaspoon cayenne pepper (optional)

Using an S blade, blend dry coconut in a food processor into a fine powder. Add nuts, salt, and cayenne; blend until the texture is a course meal. Add dates and blend; mixture should be loose, crumbly, and hold together when pressed tightly.

Press the processed ingredients firmly into a 9-inch pie plate or cheesecake pan to form the crust. Place in the freezer or refrigerator to set up while making the filling.

Filling

- 2 large avocados, peeled and chopped
- 1 tablespoon vanilla
- 1/4 teaspoon Celtic sea salt
- 1/2 cup cacao or organic cocoa powder
- 1/2 cup coconut nectar

Place all ingredients in a food processor with S blade; blend until completely smooth.

- 2 bananas thinly sliced lengthwise
- 1/2 pint of strawberries, for garnish

Divide the filling in half. Spread half of the filling in the crust. Arrange a layer of bananas on top; spread with the rest of the filling. Garnish with fresh strawberries

Refrigerate at least 1 hour before serving. This torte freezes well.

Coconut Pineapple Cupcakes

Cupcakes

- 1 cup walnuts
- 1/2 cup almonds
- 1/4 teaspoon Himalayan pink sea salt
- 1 cup unsulfured unsweetened coconut
- 1 cup Barhi or Medjool dates, pitted
- 1/4 cup coconut nectar
- 1 teaspoon pure vanilla extract
- 1/8 teaspoon freshly ground nutmeg
- 1/4 cup chopped fresh pineapple

Combine the nuts, salt, and coconut in a food processor; process into a fine meal. Add the dates, coconut nectar, vanilla, nutmeg, and pineapple to the food processor and mix well.

Use a small ice cream scoop or spoon to form balls and place in silicone muffin cups. Press the ball gently to form into a cupcake shape.

Frosting

- 1 cup cashews, soaked 1 hour
- 1/2 cup chopped fresh pineapple
- 1/4 cup coconut meat
- 1/2 cup coconut nectar
- 1 teaspoon pure vanilla extract
- 1/8 teaspoon Himalayan pink sea salt
- 2 tablespoons coconut water
- 2 tablespoons soy lecithin
- 1 tablespoon coconut oil

Combine all the ingredients, except the lecithin and coconut oil, in a Vitamix; blend until creamy. With the Vitamix running, slowly add the lecithin and coconut oil; blend until ingredients are incorporated and smooth. Put frosting in refrigerator to set up the right consistency before frosting cupcakes. Use a 10-inch pastry bag and #21 star tip to decorate cupcakes.

Decadent Chocolate Ice Cream

- 1 cup cashews, soaked 2 to 3 hours
- 1/2 cup organic coconut nectar
- 1/4 cup organic raw cacao powder
- 1 tablespoon pure vanilla extract
- 1 tablespoon sunflower lecithin or soy lecithin
- 1/8 teaspoon Himalayan pink sea salt

Combine all ingredients in a Vitamix until well blended. Pour into an ice cream freezer and mix according to manufacturer's directions.

Sesame Onion Bread

- 3 sweet Vidalia onions
- 1 cup ground sunflower seeds
- 1 cup ground golden flax seeds
- 2 zucchinis, coarsely chopped
- 1 Gala apple, cored and chopped
- 1/3 cup unfiltered extra virgin olive oil
- 2 tablespoons wheat-free tamari
- 2 tablespoons black sesame seeds

Peel and coarsely chop two of the onions. Slice the third one into very fine rings.

Combine the chopped onions, zucchini, and apple chunks in a food processor; process until very finely minced. Add the remaining ingredients to the processed mixture in a large bowl; stir well.

Spread the mixture over two or three ParaFlexx dehydrator sheets. Begin dehydrating at 110°.

In 6 hours flip and continue drying for another 4 hours. For crackers, dry for an additional 4 hours.

Store at room temperature in an airtight container or refrigerate.

Sweet Potato Pie

Crust

- 1 cup shredded dry coconut
- 1 cup macadamia nuts, cashews, almonds, hazelnuts, etc.
- 1/4 cup packed pitted dates
- 1/2 teaspoon Himalayan pink sea salt

Place dry coconut in food processor with S blade; grind into a fine powder. Add nuts and salt; blend into a texture of a course meal. Add dates and blend; mixture should be loose, crumbly, and hold together when pressed tightly. Press the crust into a 9-inch pie plate or cheesecake pan. Press firmly until the crust holds together. Place in the freezer or refrigerator to set up while making the filling.

Filling

- 3 sweet potatoes, coarsely chopped
- 1 teaspoon pure vanilla extract
- 1/2 cup coarsely chopped fresh pineapple
- 1/2 teaspoon lucuma
- 1/4 cup yacón syrup
- 1/2 cup maple syrup
- 1/4 cup coconut flakes
- 1 teaspoon cinnamon
- 1/8 teaspoon freshly ground nutmeg
- 1/8 teaspoon ground cloves
- 1/4 cup Irish moss gel
- 1/8 teaspoon Himalayan pink sea salt
- 1/2 cup coconut oil
- 1 tablespoon lecithin

Add sweet potatoes to the Vitamix; blend well. Once potatoes are broken down and blended, add all remaining ingredients into the Vitamix (except coconut oil and lecithin); blend until creamy. Slowly add the coconut oil and lecithin with Vitamix running until all ingredients are well incorporated.

Pour sweet potato mix into crust; refrigerate until the filling is set up.

Smoothies

Strawberry Lemonade Smoothie

Amazing Apple Smoothie

- 2 cups apple sauce
- 1 cup apple cider
- 1 cup orange juice
- 2 tablespoon coconut nectar
- 1/2 teaspoon nutmeg
- 1/2 teaspoon cinnamon

Combine all ingredients in Vitamix; blend until smooth.

Double Apple Smoothie

- 2 bananas
- 1 green apple
- 1 red apple
- 10 to 12 frozen strawberries
- 1 to 2 cups apple juice

Combine all ingredients in Vitamix in the order listed and mix on high until fully blended.

Apple Carrot Smoothie

- 2 cups carrot juice
- 1/2 cup organic apple juice
- 6 ounces vanilla or plain dairy-free yogurt, frozen (So Delicious brand)
- 1 banana

Combine all ingredients in Vitamix; blend until smooth.

Avocado Avalanche

- 1 large avocado, peeled and pitted
- 2 teaspoons almond milk
- 1 cup ice
- 2 tablespoons coconut nectar

Scoop out avocado into Vitamix. Add almond milk and ice; blend until semi-creamy in texture.

Banana Hazelnut Smoothie

- 4 medium bananas, peeled and sliced into 1/2 inch pieces
- 1/4 cup coconut nectar
- 1/4 cup hazelnuts
- 1 cup ice cubes
- 1/4 cup almond milk
- 1 tablespoon dark rum or hazelnut liqueur
- 2 tablespoons chopped hazelnuts, for garnish (optional)

Place the sliced bananas in a plastic bag and freeze for 1 hour. Combine all ingredients in Vitamix; blend until smooth. Garnish with chopped nuts, if desired. Serve immediately.

Banana Split Smoothie

- 1 cup almond milk
- 1 1/2 cups frozen banana slices (peeled before freezing)
- 1/2 cup pineapple chunks
- 5 strawberries, frozen
- 1 1/2 to 2 tablespoons unsweetened cocoa powder (cacao or Green & Blacks Organic)
- 2 tablespoons raw organic coconut nectar

Pour milk and coconut nectar into Vitamix. Add cocoa and fruit. Blend until smooth.

Body Machine Smoothie

- 1 cup red seedless grapes
- 3 kiwis, peeled
- 1 orange, peeled and seeded
- 1 collard leaf
- 2 leaves Romaine lettuce
- 2 cups water

Combine all ingredients in Vitamix; blend until smooth.

Cherry Cantaloupe Smoothie

- 1/2 cantaloupe, peeled, seeded, and sliced
- 1/2 cup apple juice
- 1/2 cup pitted cherries
- 1/4 cup raspberries
- 1 cup ice cubes

Combine all ingredients in Vitamix; blend until smooth.

Honeydew Mint Smoothie

- 2 1/2 cups honeydew melon
- 2 tablespoons chopped fresh mint
- 1 tablespoon fresh lime juice
- 1/3 cup water
- 1/2 cup ice

Combine all ingredients in Vitamix; blend until smooth.

Island Joe Smoothie

- 1/2 cup frozen bananas
- 1/2 cup frozen peaches
- 1/2 cup frozen strawberries
- 2 cups almond milk
- 1/4 cup orange juice
- 2 tablespoons coconut nectar

Combine all ingredients in Vitamix; blend until smooth.

Kiwi Pineapple Cooler

- 9 kiwifruit
- 2 cups pineapples
- 1/4 cup ice
- Large strawberries for garnish

Peel the kiwis and cut into small pieces. Combine all ingredients in Vitamix; blend until smooth.

Orange Pineapple Smoothie

- 1/2 cup freshly squeezed orange juice
- 1/4 cup pineapple juice
- 1/2 banana
- 1/4 teaspoon peeled ginger
- 1/2 cup ice

Combine all ingredients in Vitamix; blend until smooth.

Peaches and Dreams Smoothie

- 10 ounces organic apple cider
- 1 peach, pitted and sliced
- 6 large strawberries
- 1 banana
- 1/8 teaspoon cinnamon

Combine all ingredients in Vitamix; blend until smooth.

Pear Raspberry Smoothie

- 2/3 cup almond milk
- 1/4 cup raspberries
- 3 ripe pears, cored
- 12 ice cubes

Combine all ingredients in Vitamix; blend until smooth.

Persimmon Smoothie

- 5 persimmons, without skin and seeds
- 2 cups freshly squeezed orange juice
- 1 cup frozen berries

Combine all ingredients in Vitamix; blend until smooth.

Piña Colada Smoothie

- 1 banana, frozen (peeled before freezing)
- 1 cup almond milk
- 1 to 2 teaspoons shredded fresh Thai baby coconut
- 1/4 cup chopped fresh pineapple

Combine all ingredients in Vitamix; blend until smooth.

Pineapple Carrot Smoothie

- 1/2 cup pineapple chunks
- 1 cup unsweetened almond milk
- 1 carrot, peeled and sliced
- 1/3 cup pineapple juice
- 1 teaspoon peeled and minced ginger
- 1/4 cup coconut nectar

Combine all ingredients in Vitamix; blend until smooth.

Strawberry Blueberry Smoothie

- 1/2 cup frozen blueberries
- 1 cup frozen strawberries
- 1 banana, frozen (peeled before freezing)
- 1 1/2 cups almond milk

Combine all ingredients in Vitamix; blend until smooth.

Strawberry Lemonade Smoothie

- 1/2 cup freshly squeezed lemon juice
- 1/4 cup cold water
- 1/4 cup raw organic coconut nectar
- 3 cups sliced and partially frozen strawberries
- 1 cup ice

Combine all ingredients in Vitamix; blend until smooth.

Superfood Smoothie

- 2 organic kale leaves with stems
- 2 chard leaves with stems
- 1 tablespoon maca
- 1 teaspoon lucuma
- 1 pear
- 1 banana, frozen (peeled before freezing)
- 1 apple
- 1/4 cup goji berries
- 2 cups water

Combine all ingredients in Vitamix; blend until smooth.

Ultimate Smoothie

- 1 cup freshly squeezed orange juice
- 2 mangos, sliced
- 1 cup blueberries, fresh or frozen
- 1 banana, frozen (peeled before freezing)
- 2 tablespoons ground flax seeds
- 1 teaspoon brown rice syrup or raw organic coconut nectar

Combine all ingredients in Vitamix in order listed above. Blend on high until smooth.

Glossary

Coconut nectar: *contains 17 amino acids, minerals, Vitamin C, Vitamin B, and has a nearly neutral pH; use a 1:1 ratio to replace a liquid sweetener in any recipe; it does not have a coconut flavor*

Dulse flakes: *red seaweed harvested in the cool waters along Atlantic coast of Canada and also along the shores of Ireland and Norway; can be eaten raw, roasted, or as a thickening agent for soups*

Earth Balance: *soy-free, vegan, lactose-free, gluten-free, casein-free, non-GMO, expeller-pressed oils*

Flax seeds: *contain high levels of dietary fiber as well as lignans, an abundance of micronutrients and omega-3 fatty acids*

Goji berries: *shriveled red berries that look like red raisins which are rich in antioxidants, particularly carotenoids such as beta-carotene and zeaxanthin*

Irish moss gel: *an alternative to gelatin which is virtually calorie-less; good source of iodine, calcium, magnesium, potassium, selenium, zinc, pectin, vitamins A, B, C, E, and K, along with the essential amino acid taurine*

Jicama: *a crisp, sweet, edible root that resembles, but not related to, a turnip; a legume which grows on vines*

Lucuma powder: *a versatile sweetener that has a maple-like flavor and an excellent source of carbohydrates, fiber, vitamins, and minerals; high in beta-carotene, niacin (B3), and iron*

Maca: *a highly nutrient-dense whole food, packed with vitamins, plant sterols, many essential minerals, amino acids, and healthy fats*

Miso: *high in protein and rich in vitamins and minerals; salty, but its flavor and aroma depend on various factors in the ingredients and fermentation process*

Sunflower lecithin / soy lecithin: *contains high levels of choline, a micronutrient that is good for heart health as it breaks up cholesterol in the body; it is also vital for the proper functioning of the brain*

Tahini: *a paste of ground sesame seeds*

Tamari, wheat-free: *richer and milder taste than regular soy sauce*

Yacón syrup: *a sweetening agent, with few calories and low sugar levels, extracted from the tuberous roots of the yacón plant indigenous to the Andes Mountains*

Za'atar/Zatar: *a popular herb and spice blend of the Middle East, hand-mixed from: sumac, thyme leaves, white sesame seeds, and salt; use as a flavorful tabletop condiment*

33786697R00059

Made in the USA
Lexington, KY
09 July 2014